Australian Baby Animals

FRANÉ LESSAC

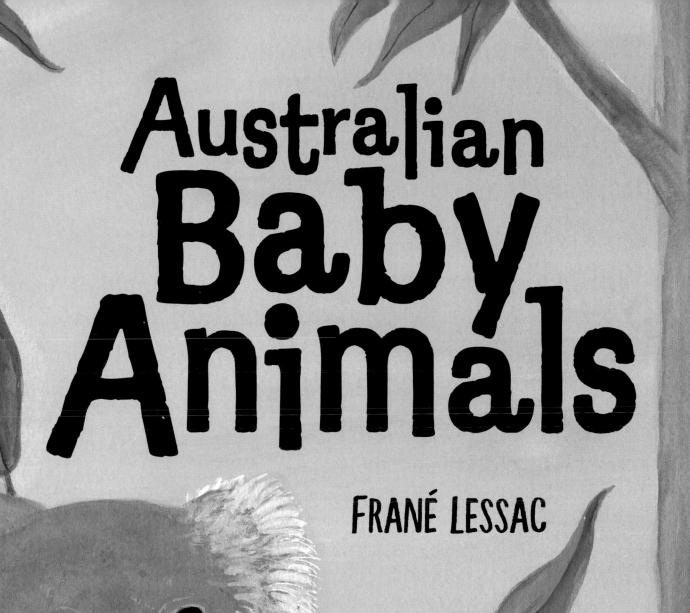

CANDLEWICK PRESS

Many Australian baby animals are called **joeys**.

A shy **kangaroo** joey plays **peekaboo** from its mom's cozy pouch.

A kangaroo's pouch keeps the joey safe and warm as its mom hops around.

A roly-poly **wombat** joey nibbles grass, staying close to its mom.

A wombat joey lives with its mom until it is about two years old.

Tiny **possum** joeys cling to their dad as he leaps from tree to tree.

The ringtail possum dad helps the mom look after their joeys.

High in a gum tree,
a sleepy **koala** joey
cuddles its mom.

A koala joey
can nap up to
twenty hours
a day.

Cheeky **Tasmanian devil**
joeys play all night long.

Sometimes, a Tasmanian devil joey will ride on its mom's back.

Some baby animals are called **hatchlings**.

Brave **crocodile** hatchlings catch a ride—they're off for their first swim.

Hang on!

Crocodile moms gently
carry their hatchlings
to the water.

Wriggly **python** hatchlings slither away, looking for a meal.

Python moms coil around their eggs to keep them warm until they hatch.

This baby animal is called a **fry**.

Teeny **sea dragon** fry
drift away from their dad.

Dad is having babies!
Sea dragon dads carry
the fry eggs on their
tails until they hatch.

These Australian baby animals are called **chicks**.

Fluffy **emu** chicks dart in and out of their dad's tall legs.

The emu dad sits on
the eggs and looks
after the chicks
when they hatch.

Noisy **cockatoo**
chicks squeal.

Feed us!

Cockatoo chicks are covered with yellow spikes that later become feathers.

Funny **kookaburra** chicks have their first laugh:

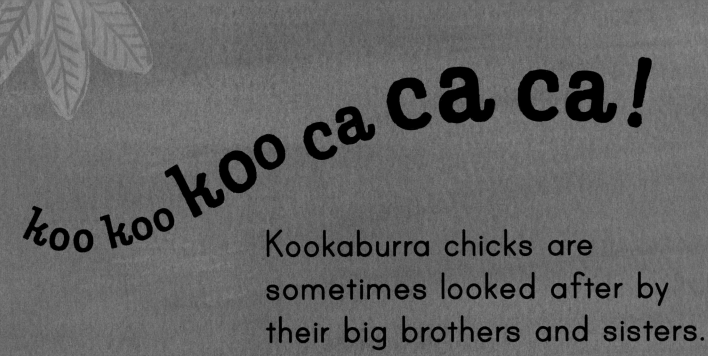

koo koo koo ca ca ca!

Kookaburra chicks are sometimes looked after by their big brothers and sisters.

This baby animal is called a **puggle**.
A hungry **echidna** puggle
is happy to see its mom.

When a puggle hatches,
it doesn't have any spines.

These baby animals are called **pups**.

A fearless **flying fox** pup holds on to its mom as she flies through the sky.

The flying fox mom wraps her wings around her pups like a blanket.

Frisky **dingo** pups race
up the desert dunes to
howl at the moon.

Dingo moms and dads hunt for food to feed their pups.

Some people call a baby platypus a **platypup**.

A clever **platypup** dives underwater, searching for a treat.

A platypup learns
to find food with its
eyes and ears closed.

hatchling

joey

chick

fry

Which is
your favorite
baby animal?

puggle

platypup

pup

For Easton, Banjo, and Miles

Copyright © 2019 by Frané Lessac

First US edition 2021
First published by Walker Books Australia 2019

Library of Congress Catalog Card Number pending
ISBN 978-1-5362-1527-4

APS 26 25 24 23 22 21
10 9 8 7 6 5 4 3 2 1

Printed in Humen, Dongguan, China

This book was typeset in Jennerik.
The illustrations were done in gouache.

Candlewick Press
99 Dover Street
Somerville, Massachusetts 02144

www.candlewick.com